WITHDRAWN

ROUNDING THE HORN

Other books by David R. Slavitt:

Poetry

Suits for the Dead
The Carnivore
Day Sailing
The Eclogues of Virgil
Child's Play
The Eclogues and the Georgics of Virgil
Vital Signs: New and Selected Poems

Novels

Rochelle, or Virtue Rewarded
Feel Free
Anagrams
ABCD
The Outer Mongolian
The Killing of the King
King of Hearts
Jo Stern

Pseudonymous novels

The Exhibitionist
The Voyeur
Vector
The Liberated
That Golden Woman
The Sacrifice

ROUNDING THE HORN

Poems by David R. Slavitt

Louisiana State University Press
Baton Rouge and London 1978

For Janet

Grateful acknowledgment is made to the editors of the following publications in which these poems appeared:

"The Vandal" in *Georgia Review*, "Lobsters" in *Mississippi Review*, "Dejeuner sur l'Herbe" in *Moment*, "House Proud" in *Choomia*, "Rounding the Horn" in *Ontario Review*, "Poison" in *Poetry*, "Night Thoughts" in *Poetry*, "Garbage" in *Hudson Review*, "Going West" in *Harpers*, and "Poster" in *Poetry*

Design: Patricia Douglas Crowder
Type face: VIP Trump Medieval
Composition: Graphic Composition, Inc., Athens, Georgia
Printer and binder: Thomson-Shore, Inc.

LIBRARY OF CONGRESS CATALOGING IN PUBLICATION DATA

Slavitt, David R., 1935–
  Rounding the horn.

  I. Title.
PS3569.L3R6   811'.5'4   78–9709
ISBN 0–8071–0458–2
ISBN 0–8071–0459–0 pbk.

Contents

I

The Vandal

With umbrella tip, spray paint, or even a chisel,
he visits upon museums his disasters,
whose name will never be listed among the masters'
nor even "of the school . . . " On the world's easel,

all he can sign is ruin. He must display,
the only way he knows, his life in art.
Restorers set to work. The damaged part
is hard to find as he is—carted away

to the proper bin, where in the day room
he talks not only of Michelangelo
but of Rembrant and Picasso, "with whom, you know,
I have collaborated," and through whom

he imagines himself as he should have been, had one
of them painted his life. The subject was right,
but he botched it, splotched and hacked at it, in spite
of the masterwork he should have been and done.

True to his pain, and seeing the choice clear—
where there can't be credit—as one between nothing and blame,
he yielded to the urge. It's like a game
in which the guards defend, lest one appear

some afternoon to score for the disgrace
of having been wounded. We all learn thus to plead
with beauty: "Though I be ugly, though I bleed,
I love you; love me, or I'll smash your face."

Killing Time

The stuff of ballads once, it now makes news
two or three times a year, of interest to
psychopathologists and those of us with a taste
for the gory. MAN SLAYS WIFE, SELF. We refuse
to dwell on it, turn the page. What have they to do
with us, such madness, hatred, excess, waste?

The super finds them, partially decayed,
after the other tenants complain, who were
disgusted that passion turns, that love goes bad
quicker than wine—and by the smell they made—
which helps to explain how he could look at her
and at himself, remember how they had

each once burned at the other's touch,
and hate what they had come to. Time's one-way
street leads only to ruin. It's no good
trying to stop or go back, however much
the best of us might yearn to or love may
deserve to. Who wouldn't if he could?

Time, then, was the villain and victim, more
than he was or she was, and its creature flesh
from which he craved release. Philosophy, art,
and all abstractions fight a guerrilla war
with time; but bullets are surer—a moment of fresh
pain and wonder, touching a vital part

and no terrible dwindling. There is no
falling away to bored indifference. Her last
stricken look was much like her first. And he
loved her more than ever, watching her go
and following, himself, into a past
tense that was better . . . It makes sense to me.

Revolutionaries

Those countless keepers of laws live, even die,
in good and decorous order, the burghers, the lords
who trust in the system and their posterity,
but a few greedy provincial workers deny
all principles of order, the accords
generations have honored, decide to be free
to thrive as they can, and, ruthless, grow and do
what the others never dared. Their creed will spread
to all the villages on the highways. New
partisans will establish their camps at the head
of the Great River. Here in the capital, all
are nervous. Rumors fly. The prices soar.
The only question is when the regime will fall
from the cancer. It is not a metaphor.

The Occupation

They leave us alone for the most part. Women shop
at their usual stores, and people go to work,
come home as they have always done, or stop
in cafes to drink and talk, but the troopers lurk

just out of sight to listen and write down
names—those they will take on their next raid.
Often, they come toward dawn, ride into town
when the sky wears that black with silver braid

of their famous uniforms. They take away
two, three, more, or sometimes only one.
We read the names in the papers the next day.
Their friends and survivors mourn and carry on:

there isn't any choice. Rage gets nowhere.
There's always the occupation, its deaths and taxes
inevitable, and we have learned to bear
its impositions. Sometimes, it relaxes,

but then it turns severe, and no one knows
what can be done but learn to live with fear.
Most of us do that. There are even those—
partisans, nuts, or both—who volunteer.

Old Woman with Cane

On a bus, a woman of seventy—what is she doing
with an adjustable cane? Do I assume three
   or four elderly ladies, or half a dozen,
all of them sharing the cane, each of them taking her turn?
   Or is there a slow cane maker, behind in his orders,
giving out loaners? No, I'm afraid it's worse. The clinic
   or agency with initials for its name,
cost-conscious in charity, must have switched over
   to this one-size-fits-all, indestructible,
ugly, but actuarily sensible metal cane
   for which men and women, boys and girls not yet
lame or even born may now be waiting, whether
   they know it or not. Observe how the woman clutches
with a liverish hand, as if to life itself, at this
   light prop of her life. It is fickle, fleeting,
likely like a bored lover to take off at any
   unfaithful moment. I suppose her husband's dead,
her children probably scattered all over the country.
   She calls them after eleven when rates go down.
They remember to call her on Christmas and on her birthday.
   This is her support. How can she bear it?
Ah, but the point is that it bears her, that she
   is no more married to it than it is to her,
And like a young girl again, she dallies, keeps it
   company only a while for she knows that another,
a gallant more dashing, more faithful is coming,
   a beau to sweep her off her halting feet
with candlelight, with flowers, with words of praise and carry
   her away. Till then, she holds on, patient,
like a great beauty stuck in a small town, passing
   the time politely with neighbors, but knowing the moment
of which she is less and less afraid will arrive to claim
   her and be claimed. She will dance away with a stranger
to take to husband at last. I pray she may. I watch
   her careful use of the cane as she gets off the bus.

The Korsakoff Syndrome

The brain pickles—it is no conceit
but happens. Dr. Korsakoff, for whom
the syndrome is named, was fascinated by
the ghostly creatures we've all seen on the street,
haunted their doorways, peered into the gloom
from which they never emerge, and with clear eye
described the bleary drunks. If their livers hold out,
they can reach a curious state of forgetfulness
for which some saints, wrestling with the doubt
that comes from lugging the body about the mess
of the world's body, have yearned, a letting go
of pride and self. There is a gentleness
these creatures have Sergei admired although
it frightened him. One may not learn to bless
from panhandlers and drunks, but one may study
their vacant look. Forgetting how to curse
is enviable. They remember their names, the brands
of cheap whiskeys—no more. If the nose is bloody,
it bothers the patient less than it does the nurse.
What happened? Blank, he stares at his dirty hands.

Eczema

Tearing at my package like a child
eager for its present, I scratch my back
between the shoulder blades, my arms, my chest,
my face, and bloody myself, like one of those wild
self-flagellating enthusiasts. The attack
subsides eventually. Exhausted, I rest

but know another episode is waiting,
another battle in this civil war
my body wages with itself. My skin
erupts periodically; it's something hating
itself, the spirit revolting at the poor
flesh it must inhabit, is trapped within.

Doctors call it a psychogenic condition,
like asthma or colitis; it is an ill
in which the skin's itch is the soul's fret,
and scratching is the body's act of contrition.
I try to absolve with an antihistamine pill
and not to get excited, not to sweat,

but there is a rage inside me, a prophet's deep
revulsion at the flesh. When it gets bad,
I scratch as in a dream of purity,
of bare-boned whiteness, clean enough to keep
the soul that's mired there now, driving me mad,
desperate, righteous, clawing to be free.

Monet

That Claude Monet developed cataracts
is terrible, yes, and one might adduce Modigliani
with his astigmatism, or Beethoven deaf,
or Smetana in the asylum, an E flat
(I think) ringing in his ears.
                              But that's all too
heroic for us. When my mother had cataracts,
could not tell if a sweater my sister gave her
was yellow or white, that was terrible too—
until the surgeon implanted a new lens
so that she can see now, read again.
But Claude Monet?
                      The dead are easy to love,
do not intrude unless invited, and never
compete. Democrat, Jacobin, Maoist can join
to mourn with mandarins, royalists, anyone
that awful vicissitude of long ago
and a man long gone.
                        We may contemplate
the peripety, that a man should be plucked up
only to be cast down again, and who can deny
a tincture of mean satisfaction. Fakirs
stare at the sun and go blind. It serves them right.
Did Monet see too much and look too hard
(harder, that is, than we look) and deserve
that opacity?
                  The March of Dimes,
Easter Seals, the Heart Association,
fighting diseases, defects, do not have
Monet in mind but us.
                          He asked one morning,
"What color is that plate?" and was told, "Blue."
"But I see it yellow."
                          It should have been dinner,
at l'Aiglon perhaps, where the chef's special is liver
and the maître is full of jokes, subtle and cruel,

but not implacable.
                    Claude Monet, too,
had an operation and saw again
blue as blue, yellow as yellow, and white
white in the justice of vision.
                              The moral is
that there is no moral.
                    Here in the Delaware Valley,
the air quality today is "unacceptable."
We must learn to breathe sparingly, to move
only when necessary. I'm sitting still,
drinking coffee. The cup in my hand is blue.

Lobsters

When lobsters lose their shells, exchange
swollen discomfort for pain and a time
of vulnerability, do they
regret their loss or find some way
to enjoy themselves until the slime
that covers their bodies, tender, strange,

becomes familiar, hardens, grows
back as protective shell to hold
the world away? Or do they mourn
that the openness with which they were born
crusts? Young again, then old,
their gray-green cautions set, enclose,

and only delicate feelers remain
to question currents, poke the ooze,
and feel and feed through another year.
Human molting is also queer:
naked now, I hated to lose
the shell I shall hate to grow again.

So after the class, the cab is late, and this time
what I've worried about all term happens: I miss
the last train, have nowhere to go, go back
(why would I go back?) to the classroom, where
they're all still there, drunk, naked,
having a fine time . . . She's going down on
him and he's eating her, and the three of them
are taking turns with her, while she and she
are off in the corner together, and I perform
my usual office, suggesting it might help some
if this leg were moved there, or that conjunction
somehow strengthened. Nobody pays attention.
I'm not surprised. Finesse will come later.
Their crude energies serve them. I wish them well.

Night Thoughts

Living quickly, mayflies and certain moths
distress us, flashing incandescent remainders
of our impending deaths. Others, slower,
tortoises for instance, or giant sequoias,
arouse our envy. We must try for balance:
admit to our lumbering bones no more of the truth
than fingernails can grasp. The hair grows;
the outer layer of skin flakes off, repairs
cuts and bruises, as scabs blossom abruptly
at the furthest promontories of the body
where the blood runs cool in Humboldt currents.

Fond of the parts of my body, I am not them,
would not become a gland to traffic in juices,
nor bone, playing the mathematics of stress,
nor eye unable to touch or move or change
the world it sees, nor even hands and feet,
those bats and moles at work in their dark silence.
Other creatures, salamanders, hippos,
algae, fast or slow, huge or tiny,
are all snug parts of the world's body,
secure as a liver or stolid as a femur.
Only the mind frets, trying to find
its right rhythm, its proper economy.
It fails sometimes, and suicide and madness
derange the innocent hands. They flutter, settle
on knife or noose or gun, flutter again,
and then fall still—except for those fingernails,
hardier, full of life, and trying longer.
Estranged, the mind is dangerous, as strangers
always are, menacing flora and fauna.

We're at our best in the morning, woolly with sleep,
or late at night, adrift among plumbing noises
when clock-time relaxes its grip. The pulse
and breath are slow enough, then, to enjoy,

quick enough to end before the glacier
returns to mark the end of eternity's wink.
There's comfort in that whiteness and cold. Alaska
will take over the world. The Fairbanks Huskies
will win the Superbowl. The last world's fair
will be Point Barrow's Expo, civilization
all in a case in the Crystal Pavilion, frozen,
and all our black sins white with snow,
even my envy of trees and fear of flies.

A man can get lost up there some days in white-outs
fifty feet from his doorstep and freeze to death.
Fifty feet from mine, sometimes, I freeze,
lost at my corner. I know what to expect.

Snake

Hiding from dawn, I burrow down in the blankets,
wake late, dawdle with coffee and the paper,
and then I feed the snake.

It is not a life I had imagined.
It is bad enough to have to feed myself,
feed and clothe my children, keep a roof over our heads,
but to carry around always this rich man's pet,
find it prey every day . . .
                                My parents were right.
This is no way to live.
But what can I do with a habit of years,
a companion of decades?
Kill it? Give it away?
They warned me this hobby of mine would prove awkward one day,
would take over my life, and it has: I watch it flick its
        tongue;
I admire its sinuous coilings and uncoilings;
I see through its old eyes; I feel its hungers.

The quick strike, the poison in the mouth,
its angle of vision, belly to the ground,
are mine now. My nerves are quickened from its study.
I divide the world now into what is edible and what is not,
what is dangerous and what is not.
People therefore avoid me, their instincts sound.
My companions are the rock I lie on,
the sun I lie in,
and of course my snake.

Even at night, its coils loop through my mind
like lianas hanging from trees I have only imagined
and strike at the small dream creatures.
Even awake, at a party, in class, on a bus,
I feel it rattling, ready.

Eve was right. The snake is fascinating.
And she had never before seen dissimulation,
the beginning of mimesis, the start of art.
Who would not choose to go on the road, live by her sweat,
play where she can, rather than stay in a garden
where every bush is nakedly real,
conceals nothing, implies nothing behind it,
hints nothing in its shadow?

Sick to death of the obviousness of facts,
the crude truths of polity and ambition
as well as love and death as they actually happen,
Cleopatra turned for aid, for relief, to an asp,
for snakes promise us new life and fresh starts,
imaged as hoops, holding their tails in their mouths—
an exaggeration of how they slough old skins
to slide out bright as new.
She wanted that.

Cassandra's ears were said to be serpent licked,
the snake's kiss in Apollo's temple
opening her to the gift.
My snake, too, sometimes finds surprising truths,
sliding around in his yellow and green cage,
finds them and gobbles them up to lie, bulging,
content for a while, and willing to let me rest
at least until the hunger comes back to rouse him
to rouse me to the hunt
in the tall grass.

Putting on Heirs

The heir a detestable brother, and the estate
entailed it did not require very great
imagination to plunge into debt, to deck
the hall with mortgages. The real flair
was in the spending, to make an enduring wreck
of the brother's hopes and let him be merely heir
to dazzling ruin. Therefore, rather than booze
or horses, the safe conventional ways to lose,

the viscount plowed his thousands into the grounds,
constructing terraces, vistas, scattering pounds
like leaves, like blades of grass, to make a Versailles
in Ireland, a uselessness to bloom
for decades, affronting the undelightful eye
of that dreary sibling, Lewis, the dolt to whom
the Powerscourt title and land would have to pass
when the viscount was planted beneath his expensive grass.

He hired Robertson who rode around
in a wheelbarrow, drinking, while he turned the ground
into an earthly Eden. Every day,
when the bottle was finished, so was Robertson. Art
demands a lot. A patron learns to pay
attention as well as money. A joke at the start,
the work turned into something else, took root
in the tricky soil of the passions, and bore fruit.

The brother, the spite, forgotten, the Irish lord
made arbors, groves, and gardens he couldn't afford,
hired the county's farmers, a godsend
to them and the money lenders of the day.
A fool, they thought, a madman—or a friend
to Ireland, but he didn't care what they
said about him. The gardens were his life—
or so he thought until, at last, his wife

of sixteen years surprised him with a son,
an heir to all this folly. What he'd done
was senseless now. That ruin he had planned
preferred him to his brother and settled there
like an old retainer. He, busy with grand
schemes, continuations, and the rare
shrubs he was importing, ignored it. So?
What happened to them all? Do we want to know?

From the brother, perhaps relief and probably scorn;
from the wife—for herself and the children (five were born)—
rage, I should think, which, after a few years,
the youngsters learned for themselves, disappointment and greed
having been sung into their little ears
like lullabies. Did the viscount pay them heed?
Or walk his garden, where plants, wherever he went,
were silent, grateful, profligate with content?

Let the lofty views of trees distract him. Let
patterns clarify that no eye yet
can see but in which his grandchildren will live.
Let light answer to shade, and showers of gold
amaze even the prudent who will forgive
if not applaud extravagance so bold.
And let him stand still beneath an oak that sways
but slightly to the yammering of jays.

Landscape Artists

The gardens, greenswards, and all the carefully tended
prospects of madhouses, insisting that order,
beauty, and calm can exist anywhere, must
be therapeutic. Even the best-defended
loony, hiding deep in his wilderness,
must be sometimes tempted. Across the border,
there are fountains, flower beds. In my distress,
stung by my jungle's bugs, I long to trust
that vision of the gardeners and the shrinks,
and would, except that, cowering in my lair,
I know that open spaces are risky. The sun
sets, the cat prowls, the owl blinks,
and under the close-clipped bushes, blood and hair
punctuate what those gardeners have done.

Pour l'Election de son Sepulchre

Entelechies are deaths. Lear's, for example,
completed him and his action in the kingdom
of consequence where each of us is sovereign.
(Nahum Tate did not understand this, let
Lear live, doing him the violence
of a mortuary cosmetician.)
                              Thinking
of death, and reading late at night, while sirens
cry like predatory birds, the word
roams the rooms of my head, an unlaid ghost.
The last judgment is easier: someone else,
or something else, decides—angels, rabbis,
celestial lawyers, wrangling their disputes
out of my hands. Entelechy, more abstract,
is also more personal, my own business.
Assume in this muddle some possibility
of order, a resolution I cannot imagine
but may yet grow into or sink into,
losing extraneous detail, coming clear.
Magic has failed: Prospero's books, or Faust's,
discarded at the end, offer us nothing.
The spells that work are the obvious. Everyone knows
that this is what there is, and entelechies
like some good photographs start here, end here,
but manage to satisfy by the light, the grain,
or the simplicity some primitive tribes fear,
seeing them all death masks. More civilized
we like, nevertheless, on our dust jackets
mug shots, brimming essences.
                              Intellect,
tired of complications, turns on itself,
longing to love or hate, longing to rest
in certainties. Death is one of those.

II

The Later Ptolemies

Disintegration, distraction . . .
                              It is the time
of the later Ptolemies: the same laws, the same
temples, even the same good will of Soter,
or Philadelphus, the wish above all things
for the happiness of the subjects . . .
                              It didn't work.
The same enlightened regimen was without effect
for Philopator, Epiphanes, for Philometor
and for his brother Physcon.
                              Economics teases,
tantalizes with reasons, suggests a process
that is more than a glum narrative.
Its assumptions are Soter's—that reason and good will
can solve any problem
                       Later, they learned better.
It is enough to say that my life, our lives, these times
have gone bad.
                  Religious novelties,
fanatics of the temples and of the streets
kick the machine to make it spit candy.
The machine is broken, the repairman dead.

There may be some, a fortunate few,
who are happy, who call themselves happy,
who keep to their homes, growing their own comforts.
I cannot name more than three.
I am not sure of those.
Bad times and worse coming.
I grieve for the children but, more, I grieve for the old
who remember better.
                       The Talmudists say of death
that it is "very good."
                       I say a man's life
is a long session of study to crack that tough nut
and chew its kernel.
The bitter taste fades and at last turns sweet.

Jeremiad

What walls our grandfathers labored to build,
and our fathers to mend, are fallen.
Gaps larger than gates gape.

The volumes they collected are tattered, scattered,
all overdue. There are no new acquisitions.
Not even foundation officials read
the studies of indifference and boredom they have funded.

The schools offer advanced degrees
in dilettantismo. The pursuit of pleasure,
distracted clergymen say, is a legitimate way.

Who can accept this?
Who can struggle against it?

Polite, we try to entertain one another,
having agreed never to allude
to what we all know:
That the times require a stern prophet.

Were one to appear,
he would, if shrewd, take an ad in the "Personals" column,
with a box number for passionate replies.

A Dirge for Lord Paget

From France, Paget, the well deserving Lord,
of Beaudesert, wrote the Earl of Warwick:
" . . . having no friend to succour us, destitute
of money to furnish us, and so far in debt
as hardly we can find any creditors . . . "
Oh, give up, and let their orgueil swallow
Boulogne. Still we shall have Calais. Money
debased, morals gone with the gospels' coming,
the lands enclosed for sheep and against good yeomen . . .
But with a peace, a little space of peace,
we can make amends.
                        A sane policy . . .
Which of us dares believe it enough to get up,
put on the morning's harness, and fight another
day?
        On raked gravel, Manzu's cardinals
loom, their capes and copes perfect cones,
their faces minimal lines as I imagine
Paget's face that gave away nothing
to Rochpot.
                Except Boulogne.
                                The Renaissance
presumed all cardinals damned for their luxury,
power, and pride, as we believe all statesmen
scoundrels, senators, governors, judges whoremasters
and thieves. From dirty worldliness we flinch,
retreat to dreams of heaven, of love, of a lost
past . . .
            "The time is turned," said Paget. "Then
was then, and now is now."
                            Admit it. Yield.
Put on the formal court costume. Brave
those long halls. We make what deals we can,
good or bad. Those men believed in something:
the world in front of their eyes and under their feet.

Louis

Bernard the bastard got Italy, was king of Italy,
but if a natural son could be king of anywhere,
why not emperor of Everywhere? Uncle Louis,
younger son of Big Charlie, to move up
from Aquitaine? No, order is order,
and the firstborn of the firstborn should inherit.
Let him stay in Aquitaine!
                                          Bernard rebelled,
and lost—battle, throne, eyes, and life,
not having survived the rough procedure
ordered by uncle, him called in Italy
Louis the Pious, and in France, the Debonair.
A hard business, even for Pedro the Cruel.
But for softness is he damned, historians having
"in general more indulgence for splendid crimes
than weaknesses of virtue." Big Charlie's
organization shattered. Louis let it go
with "a conscience too strict, a temper too soft."
Bernard couldn't see it, but there it was:
Verdun, the treaty of 843, the map of Europe,
that mess of a thousand years.
Difficult lessons, but a little blood
may save more, rivers of it spilled
for virtue, for conscience.
Grab, grind 'em down. When they say, "Uncle,"
smash them, and keep on. No ruler
but one who knows how to kill.
Our sufferings come from gentle men
who hesitate, the writhing beyond
their mediocre imaginations. Strike
clean, and don't look back. Sirs,
we recognize these truths, know them at night,
but dare not tell our children in the daylight
what Charlemagne, who should have, never
taught his pious, debonair, ruinous son.

Glaucus

"But Zeus
had stolen Glaukos' wits away—
the young man gave up golden gear for bronze,
took nine bulls' worth for armor worth a hundred."
—*The Iliad*, VI (Fitzgerald trans.)

What's the difference? All the gold in the world,
that solid eighteen-yard cube, isn't worth a thing
to a dead man. Lord Diomedes' bronze
could keep a spear point, sword edge, arrow head
from flesh and blood better than Glaucus' gold.
It's a better than even swap, friend. Take it!
Your life, and even your life with honor, for gold.
And Glaucus did, keeping his wits and head
on his shoulders to drive, alive, from the field into Troy.

My kind of man. But what's the difference? Later,
at the Greek wall, where not even great Lord Hector
could move against the rampart, Lord Sarpedon,
crazed with a holy hunger, a lion famished
for glory, hefts a pair of spears and speaks
to Glaucus, his cousin, his friend. And Glaucus listens:
    Biddledeegoo giddledeebah diddledeebee
    Honor giddledeeboo vines and fields
    Biddledeegah duty biddledeegee
    Wives children giddledeebah glory
    Deathless biddledeegoo we will attack!
So Sarpedon spake, the morning sun
kindling fire behind him, and on the wall
Menestheus, hearing it, scared shitless, hollered
for help, any help he could get—Tall Ajax,
Little Ajax, any Ajax, Teucros,
anybody, but quick . . .
                  but held the position
as long as he had to, waiting for help to come.

And they do come, the Telemonian Ajax
and Teucros, the bowman. Ajax kills Epicles,
smashing his brains with a rock, and Teucros shoots
Glaucus in the arm. He falls from the wall . . .

What's the difference? Sarpedon fights, and Hector
breaches the gate at last.
                              Gold, bronze,
honor, wives, country, giddledeeboo
biddledeegah giddledeebee
                              Death
turns it all into nonsense, dulls the shine,
quiets the shouting.
                    He bought himself some time
(what else have we got?) worth all the bulls in the world.

House at Anvers by Van Gogh

The house in the title is in the distance, the wall
four fifths of the way up the canvas. Below,
closer, is grass, yellow-green and green
palette-knife slashes, a savage expanse
that makes the white wall and the white house
a refuge, suggests a calm or a relief
for which it is almost folly even to hope.
There are no tricks with light. In stillness and motion,
with texture and placement, the house is made secure,
the separating emptiness appalling.

We get along with what we have and manage
to adjust the frame of what we can expect,
but a chance vista can cut, the field of vision
dance with longing, shimmer with chagrin
we do not understand for something we had,
lost, and cannot remember, or something we wanted
and were sure would make us happy, whatever it was:
nobody has to ask what's in that house.

Four Quatrains

1
Green wood, I smoked and sizzled;
new wood, and I smoldered;
seasoned now, dry wood,
I burn with tongues of fire.

2
Lucid skies, a proportionate wildflower blue,
gave way as the weather turned to riverfog, groundfog:
barns, neighbors' houses, fences softened, bulged
with driads, naiads, nereids, looking like you.

3
Before the approach of the northern hordes,
the mandarin, too, fled, but in his pack,
with his writing brush and his flute,
he carried more of the city than oxen could lug.

4
Your terrible secret will sort out your friends
or scatter them all away. To whom dare you speak?
Alone, at a quick-lunch counter, you don't even remember
who sat where at your oval feasting table.

Manifesto

A stone the right shape,
a skillful boy, and with luck . . .
three skips on water.

So poems skip. I
have practiced with many stones
and trust now to luck.

It demands spirit,
or rather the stubborness
to keep on trying

when everyone else,
grown up, moves on to other
more sensible work.

OOOOOO
_____

The fathers say
that all our sins
will wash away
in the blood of the lamb.
It may be so,
and we will know
one day. Till then,
we mortal men,
poor sinners all
since Adam's fall,
must pray and look
in the world's book
to find some sign,
as I have, mine.
An odometer's row
of nines will go
around to naught,
as the car, new-bought,
showed at the start.
Creator, Healer,
Maker, Dealer,
Lord, let my heart
turn back to a fine
Eden of Zeroes,
assembly-line
clean; let me
be covered again
by warranty.

Nudes

Gothic painters' scrawny
Eves and Adams shrank from
a Platonist Creator.
All Platonists are prudes.
Stripped of old religious
habits, we can bask in
the Renaissance's passion
for fleshly, pagan nudes.

The history of art yields
many such examples:
vision is a function
less of eye than mind.
Revolutionary
courage was required
before we learned to look on
beauty's bare behind.

But figurative painting
has fallen out of fashion.
The epidermal surfeit
of summer's seaside scenes
has driven to abstraction
those odalisques, who sulk now
on fold-out color pages
of certain magazines.

As distant grass grows greener,
so flesh is rounder, pinker,
hair softer, the lips fuller,
and the eyes a brighter blue
when beauty is forbidden,
glimpsed barely, or imagined,
and not the nude who's likely
to wake up next to you.

Still, we ought to offer
thanks for the suggestive
jostle. Greeks assumed that
the stranger in a crowd,
whose beauty was a kick in
the solar plexus, might be
Aphrodite, come down
from her Olympian cloud.

Soap Opera

They wade through sorrows scriptwriters devise
in kitchens, hospital rooms, divorce courts, jails,
or cemeteries, and nearly everyone tries
to do the right thing. And everyone fails.

Their happiness is only a setup for woe.
Fridays are always bad—although the mood
is seldom brighter than desperate—and they go
staggering on to Monday's vicissitude.

Stupid, I used to think, and partly still
do, deploring the style, the mawkishness.
And yet, I watch. I cannot get my fill
of lives as dumb as mine: Pine Valley's mess
is comforting. I need not wish them ill.
I watch, and I delight in, their distress.

Adaptation from Callimachus

Book club selections, interstate four-lane
roads, school-hall fountains, and fall
homecoming queens . . . any public thing
disgusts me. Thus, I must explain
my tepid attitude, lovely and tall
as I admit you are. Should I bring
a gift, ask if you're home, my dear,
hope for gloria in excelsis,
and wait downstairs, I'll surely hear
you're in—and also somebody else is.

Misogynist Poem

from Palladas of Alexandria
(*Greek Anthology*, IX, 166)

Woman upright, or woman flat on her back—
bad news either way. Homer shows us so:
from round-heeled Helen, the *Iliad*, Troy's wrack;
from chaste Penelope, all of the *Odyssey*'s woe.
Either way, a woman is ruin. Flee
from anybody who sits down to pee.

Youth, Age, Life, and Art

Innocent, young, I wove syntactical nets
to snare moments of joy, but when one gets
older, the trick is reversed, and, late at night,
to fend the beasts off—fear, rage, and despair—
that prowl the dark or hover in the air,
I sit in my circle of lamplight and I write.

Sunshower

Cloud overhead and its rain falling wind-slanted,
and the sun beveling light from the west in, under,
the rain and sun meet in spattering glints
so the air is at war and the grass is a battlefield,
the wet and the light colliding, and tree leaves shaking,
alarmed as their two sources of life skirmish,
pelt one another, and fall to earth as if wounded.
Like a tree or a fool, I stand in the sunshower's tracers,
and shine in the dazzle, dazzled. A trick of the weather,
but I can remember moments of my own weather,
as chancy, smaller than this, and passing as quickly,
when laughter and tears warred on my wet face,
and thrashed in the branches and leaves of my life, the sun
slanting down one way, and rain falling another.

Pumpkin Men

Not for the children who do not believe
(perhaps for the children we were, or want to have been),
we fashion pumpkin men, and out on the lawn,
or porch, or even up on the roof

perch these figures: harvest gods.
It isn't for what they will do. There are no toys
to funnel down our chimneys, bags of sweets,
the protection money our spooks extort.

The gifts have already been received.
We have lived to see our trees ringed by another
year, the bud green of desire grown
to the gold of wealth and pumpkins.

If we were children, we should know
the god of all this, how to entertain,
to offer a chair, thanks, how to perform
simple devoirs and not feel foolish

as the shabby figure up on the roof
and as out of place, for both of us condescend.
The pumpkin men, here on sufferance, suffer
our discomfiture as frosty prayer.

Dejeuner sur l'Herbe

Assume some minimal order on the planet,
some principle of equity, and grant
an apple is potent as a pomegranate,
and look to the bee, thou dullard, as well as the ant.

Two bites from the apple they weren't to eat,
and then, in the awful moment, they let it fall
to the grass of paradise where all its sweet
juice oozed a rich olfactory call

to our constant picnic friends. The red and the black
ants shared the taste and therefore the fate
we have long mourned together, and from the trees,
one, then a few, then a swarm of sweet-toothed bees
joined the al fresco feast, were turned out of the gate,
and like us yearn, remember, want to go back.

Only having eaten more, having gorged and finished
the whole thing, they learned more than we.
The orderly hills of the ant and the hives of the bee
are like our towns, but even less diminished

suburbs of the City of God. They commute
from innocence to nuisance, and they still
continue searching, haunt our picnics, and will
until they find another piece of that fruit.

Tristram

If there were only the snore of the prow
to fear, the sound that giddies the ear,
or the Irish coast of which to steer
clear, or a potion, or silly vow,
life would be safer, but pavement can fall
or heave into billows. This punch tastes queer.
I hear that rushing sound. I hear
you ask me, "Do you know Cornwall?"

In Poland, Pigs

Having roughly the body weight of humans,
the pig is a subject for tests of various kinds—
of drugs, for example, but also of man's (and woman's)
aspirations. All of us turn our minds

to heaven, hope for justice, pray that the swine
who cheated us, who checked us on this earth,
will suffer punishments, undergo such fine
tortures, we cannot imagine them; that our worth

will be recognized; that the meek will be blessed, the last
promoted first, and the mighty be brought low.
We wish, try to believe, and we hold fast
to such old and pleasant texts as promise so.

In Poland, pigs—or some of them—are dressed
in burlap suits, while others in the sty
wallow naked. Why should some be blessed,
tricked out in relative finery, and why

should others fare less well? The questioning pig,
assuming such a creature, would not understand
the obvious truth if he heard it. (One need not dig
for truth as sows do for truffles.) The grand

couture is perfectly practical. It protects
the pigs' skins, keeps them from getting scarred—
not for this pig's world, but for the next,
for the curriers' and the wallet makers' hard

scrutiny, and their customers', who demand
quality goods. The pigs know nothing of this
and do not pray. They do not understand
peace or justice, or try to imagine bliss.

Poster

That it was cheap was not the only reason;
even for free, who needs a *Vogue* poster
of a lady in a long dress and a large hat
with a flowing veil, riding—sidesaddle, of course—
a rearing zebra?
        There must have been something, three
dollars' worth of message units, speaking
to our slight impulse. Do I believe in her
elegance that sits upon wildness, rides it,
and draws upon it? Is the farouche chic?
But, no, she would be smiling. Her face is clearly
wistful—and the zebra, rearing, is trying
to throw her off, run free, and join the three
giraffes in the middle distance. Her seat is sure,
though under the long green skirts we may imagine
the muscles of her slender thigh tensed,
feel them straining in the bizarre dressage
of animal and spirit. Those contradictory graces
are joined in equipoise: the zebra's strength,
the power of that striped haunch, that arched neck,
dissipates into her veil; and she is sorry,
knowing as the beast cannot, how long
their ride must be. She can never dismount,
can never be thrown . . .
        He could canter off
to fall to a hungry lioness, and she
could grow fat, perhaps, and old, no doubt, and gossip
at the watering places of fashion.
        But, no, she knows
she is only a poster, the hot hide under her ass,
a Platonic idea of lust. An idea blows
her veil; a real wind coming off the mountains
would whip the damned hat off . . .
        If only it would!
Then something could happen—even something dreadful.
Which is to say, she doesn't believe in the zebra,

cannot imagine him, any more than he
has any idea what's up there on his back
but a body in a world of bodies, a beast
like him. He is certainly not impressed
by the silly beads about her neck, her shawl
of gauzy lime-green stuff. The bridle is real,
horse-hide or cow-hide, and the bit in his mouth
tastes of metal. He wants to spit it out.
His hoof marks scar the earth in dumb rage.
     Of course, they're together, then, innocent, gorgeous,
fighting to master each other and the picture,
and each needing the other. If the wind
were real it would come alive and end in an instant
to serve, stopped frame, as an image of earthly love.

Air for Xylophone

The clown is supposed to be sad, but what about
    the xylophone player
who has more reason, must come, sooner or later,
    to realize how wanting
in culture or common sense his parents were
    (or, worse, her parents
were) to permit, to purchase so absurd,
    so vulgar an instrument,
and who, moreover, must have had to practice,
    for unlike the clown,
the xylophone player does not try to be funny,
    but alone in her
(yes, it has to be her) room plinky-plonks
    through long afternoons
with a wooden zest only a moron or lunatic
    would be likely to feel . . .
Or, dare we assume a reasonable world
    or even one
reasonable person who, deliberately,
    took up that grotesque
instrument, studied, practiced—not to perform
    or for any crass
reason like a career, but in expectation
    that sometime a time
of foolish pleasure, pure glee would arrive
    when nothing else
could possibly serve to capture, to cap the mood,
    no laugh or giggle
be adequate, and then, walking across the room
    to that silly instrument
forethought or happenstance had put or left there,
    under the window
or perhaps next to the bed for the instrumentation
    of just this occasion
she could pick up the hammers, lean forward, and let
    loose the right,

the perfect jumpy, flashy, xylophone riff?
        Probably not. Instead,
she is condemned to it, lugs it about,
        a musical millstone;
eventually, if she is sensible, she
        gives it up,
and when that moment arrives, regets, more
        than the rest of us
would, that nothing is there in the corner, no
        keys to pound,
no semi-primitive notes for her to strike
        in the turbid air,
or perhaps that appropriate moment never arrives . . .
        But is that worse?
To be prepared for the transport of delight,
        the astonishing moment,
the mere anticipation of which keeps most
        of us living going?
How bad can life, the world be, if there are still
        xylophone makers
working in ateliers, in the side streets.
        Should the Messiah
come it is no more likely that he will ride
        a white donkey
than that he will come playing the xylophone.

Pitcher

More than itself,
more even than a globe, a mere map,
the ball he holds is all our histories
made palpable, our fears and ambitions
wound on themselves and stitched roughly
in Haiti in horsehide,

a hunter's stone
civilized to a plaything for games.
Serious fans keep their eyes on the ball;
we, dilettantes, watch the man, the motion
on the mound, that of a slingshot
on a catapult. He

throws himself on
each pitch, aims not at the plate, not at
the catcher's inviting mitt, so much as
at a backstop of the limits of man's
grace, his living of his body
like that of a woman.

See, on the mound,
how he pauses, gathers his spirits,
defies time that will wither his arm, take
the hop off his fastball, the break off curves,
the obedience of objects
and the flesh to his will.

Older pitchers,
crafty, pot-bellied, capture our hearts
as some older women do—a Lolich

or a Tiant, still with the stuff, daring
the threat of each bat to the row
of virginal zeros,

relying on
wiles, substitutes for a while for the
speed of a Fidrych fireball. They throw junk,
go with what works until, from the bullpen,
the long reliever takes over.
The rare perfect game is

negative, pure.
We swill beer and yearn for such a world
to be real in which talent, effort, and
strength can achieve innocence, even an
inning's unsullied grace, we with
our lousy E.R.A.s.

Black Hole

Dark clouds scud overhead and threaten
dull afternoons, arthritic pains, and rain,
while farther out, other, darker clouds
threaten worse or promise better, shrinking
to densities fertile as mud in which blue stars
sprout like periwinkle, crocus, hydrangea.

They used to be fixed, whirling in Ptolemy's circles
or even in Kepler's odd but certain ellipses,
and looking up on summer nights was soothing.
We see better now, and in monstrous dishes
culture mortality—white dwarf and black hole
are eventual, like the deaths of our parents. Passions,
ambitions startle the air like fountains of gas
out of the dark that fall back into the dark.

The Animal Act

Of course he knows what he's doing. The gun at his hip
is mostly for show, and when he cracks his whip,
it's to catch our flighty attention as much as that
of the graceful, silent, dangerous, lazy cat
perched on its little pedestal, blinking at him,
about to jump again through the hoops of his whim
and of our morality pageant in which rage
and lust may roar but lope back to their cage
every time to doze between shows. We know
its dreams of flesh, fear them, and would not go
into that ring for anything. Overhead,
an aerialist, blindfolded, plays our dread
for all it's worth, treading the high wire
above the lion's cage. Just so, desire
and fear in balance keep our feet on the straight
line of our intentions that keeps our weight
from gravity's jaws, or nature's. Or the beasts'
of the maximum circus for whom we are feasts.
Whatever roars or growls or screams in the pits
below the arena is eager to tear to bits
our delicate pretensions. The Romans' odds
were long but fair; they lived with what the gods
decreed, knowing that big cats are disaster
a few can fend off but no one can master.
In play, for fun, they maul, meaning no harm,
but a friendly swat of a paw can break your arm.
An affectionate lick of their rough tongues can take
your skin off. They sleep a lot but wake,
feel their animal spirits, and want to frisk
with their pals, their trainers, who accept the risk
as one of their rewards, knowing love's dangers.
We watch in the center ring an encounter of strangers,
of man and animal, in each other's spell,
and thrill, and worry, and pray they come out well.

Reunion Elegiacs

Twenty years ago, we all had dreams;
now we come back to what we recognize is a dream
    of intelligent good will. The lies we swap
cannot conceal the truth, which is hypertense, fat,
    running to baldness, nor hide the graver defects
of spirit, for we have all more or less botched our lives,
    and those to whom we might like to apply for forgiveness,
encouragement or understanding retired or died
    years ago. In familiar buildings, strangers
speak only to the young in that language of wise assurance
    we shall never again hear. Our simple tricks
we take for granted: no longer are we much surprised
    to be earning livings. Instead, there is hurt and rage
at careers going bad, at sickness, divorce, death, at age
    which should leave such fine, such promising young.men,
as all of us are, alone. We and catastrophe
    ought to have nothing in common. Whatever became
of amusing land-grant colleges, producing grist
    for the mills of disappointment? Or turn it around
and ask, if we are the best, the most fortunate of men,
    how the others must live, and how they bear it.
Now that we know the questions and yearn for answers,
    our masters are gone. None is left to guide,
help, hint, or moderate the unfair assignment.
    Nothing stands between us and the great stumper—
What is the good life?—which is why we come back,
    repair to these sturdy battlements, and try
to regain some of the brashness (never mind the joy)
    with which we made our good beginnings here.

But the hot breath of two decades, both of them bad,
    has fogged the glass, has blurred the delicate image
of what an education, a life ought to be.
    Who is not in favor of civil rights
or against war? Such choices are easy, indeed vulgar,
    as all public issues and public men

seem now. When Eisenhower spoke on the green,
    a few of us went to see him, to view a relic,
a hero with aphasia and a "What, me worry? " grin.
    We could not know that he was one of our masters,
presiding over us more than Whitney Griswold could,
    letting us alone, letting us be.
Since then, the charlatan, villain, crook, and now the fool
    have taken their turns, each turn worse than the last
screwing. Involvement gave way to anger, gave way to disgust
    for those who followed us. Our sons and daughters,
for whom we had hoped, to whom we had looked for better,
    are here now, standing in our old places,
less comfortably, less fortunately than we stood,
    their prospects diminished from ours. We grieve for them,
discover, too late, how happy we were, and find out we share
    a quality of dreaming they can't have.
We carry with us, sirs, the burden of better days
    we did not deserve, but for which we now must pay
if only by remembering how it was, by keeping
    some of the grace and assurance of our youth
alive in us. We meet again like a tribe of exiles,
    unprepossessing perhaps, but in our demeanor
proud because we remember, and know how to hope for, a better
    time than this. Our duty, for God and country,
and Yale, too, is survival. I wish us all well.

    Thrive and prosper, so that our hearts' spores
may be preserved for the chance of a change in the world's weather.
    Some of us, in some more carefree season,
may blossom yet again, to show what it is to be happy,
    to demonstrate that intelligence, good will,
and all our nameless graces can never quite disappear.
    Battered as we may seem, we're the golden boys,
still fortune's darlings, who once roistered here,
    blessed: it is up to us in turn to bless.

III

House Proud

The haughty columns cost. The Cape Cod painter
calls them "pillows," and every four or five years
slaps white paint on them from scaffold work.
Each pillar takes a gallon.

I have fixed the metal strip on the front door threshold.
The screws had rusted smooth and the strip had risen
so the door caught on a screw head, wouldn't close right.
The cut glass window panes were in danger, the old putty,
dried out, was falling away with the slamming.
I have reputtied the window panes.

It is a long process, a continuing struggle
against decrepitude. There are timbers in the barn
that are rotted, that must be replaced this year,
that should have been done last year. The back hall skylight
leaks again in heavy rains.
I must see to it.

There are practical reasons for doing these things.
Costs go up. Repairs are a part of the investment—
if I think of the house as an investment.
It has value. I can borrow on it,
but its value is other than what can be measured in dollars.
After a time, a house is part of one's body.
One learns the places to duck on the back stairs,
the spaces the furniture lives in, can pass through rooms
at night without lights, feeling the air,
knowing the feet, the legs, the arm rests of chairs
as surely as one knows the length of one's own stride,
the bulk of the body itself,
for the house is a part of the body,
and the body is part of the body of the house.
The process of bruising and healing goes on,
except for the intervention of age and of lean years
when mending is slower or stops altogether.

The house is older than I am, older
than my father, stood here before my grandfather
came to this country, before my grandfather was born.
He died before I was born.

But I have planted the dogwood, have planted the euonymus,
the viburnum and the azaleas, put in the mimosa tree
and the flowering hawthorne and the flowering quince.
I cut down the hemlocks and spruce that darkened the side porch
and put in the juniper bushes I have to keep clipping.
The elms were here before, were here before the house.
The two in front sicken, dying. The one out in back
is still all right, and, far away enough,
may stay all right.
I hope it will stay all right.

The body's failures at first are slight and even endearing,
the lines around the mouth and the eyes suggesting domestic
pleasures and pains passed but not wholly forgotten,
the thickening at the waist and the droop of flesh
at the chin and around the upper arms more cozy than woeful,
until one day it has all gone too far, has turned slatternly, squalid,
and beyond repair. The fastidious soul frets,
lingers awhile in a growing discontent,
and then sells out, packs up, moves away—
some say to a better neighborhood
in another town.

There used to be a pond in front of the pillars.
The house looked out over three descending terraces
to the pond and across the water and hill to the town
and the church steeple, a white that matched its own.
The pond was drained in the eighties or early nineties,
turned to a bog for cranberries, was abandoned,
turned to a swamp, turned to a landfill plot
for new houses that haven't yet been built.

A gracious prospect diminished, then repaired
as spruce and birch and a beech tree filled the spaces,
made a green wall, a small wood
on the lower terraces.
The view is shorter,
but here and there, sometimes, nature is healing,
prospects change, and we adapt our lives,
turn around. One door closes. Another,
the one that leads to the dining room for instance,
opens, as traffic flows in new ways
on the old floor boards.

What less or what better
can we hope for ourselves or for those we love?

Four Sonnets

1 Packing
Packing again, I find old goodies—a pen,
a hat, a cigarette lighter I'd lost, but not
the sanguine hopes I brought to this place when
I moved here. Along the line somewhere, forgot,
missing, I had a notion once of a new
life . . . Bloodied now, I've let that go
and wander around the way Laplanders do
following reindeer's beastly whims, although
those animals feed the Laps while mine are good
for nothing. Still, there's no other life around,
no reason to stay. I'm moving on,
and know what I'll find—another part of the wood,
and something to trap, to kill, until the ground
is wasted like this, like me, all the game gone.

2 Moving
With the books piled in toppling towers, the clothes
spilling out of suitcases like Jews
clamoring for visas, the place is a shambles
on which we've stumbled, anthropologists
studying how a civilization crumbles . . .
Easily, easily! We can make plans, make lists—
we need a cutting board—and figure the costs
in effort and dollars of righting things for a time,
and may succeed. A month from now, what's lost
will mostly be replaced. The apartment will seem
comfortable, nearly secure against the ghosts
we are sure we've shaken. Nothing is the same.
What is here to hurt us? Disconsolate,
a lone shoe in a closet mourns its mate.

3 Auto-Suggestion
The blacktop ahead shimmers as if it were water,
the landscape rises slightly on both sides
on a road I have never driven, though others like it

have mapped my life. All roads are the same.
Trees close by loom up and disappear,
desires; others, up on the crest of the hill,
hold on the horizon, ideas of trees.

What kind of law is that, what kind of perspective
for close objects to vanish while distant stay?
What trick of optics turns the future liquid
melting the ground? Only the middle distance
is recognizable, solid ahead, branches
waving of real trees that follow along
on left and right. We live in the middle distance.

4 The Old House
To return, to be redeemed, to play again
in whatever fields of the Lord we can recall
of youth, of home, of Eden, such is the prayer
that crackles through the ether from all men
and women for whom the idea of the fall
has nothing to do with a couple, Gothic, bare,
posturing in a pictured glade, but sets
one room, one time, against another. The wish
is always to go back. We can't. Regrets
fill up the cup, congeal upon the dish
salvaged from that other life that's gone.
I wince to see it. Last week, I drove by
the old house. New owners carry on
the messing up we started, you and I.

Walking the Dog

A dog will sniff at bushes, newel posts,
a familiar ivy bed, track his own scent,
and lift his leg wherever it seems right
to sign his claim. In pride of place he boasts,
"My territory!" And we pay our rent
and use the pot (until then, it's not quite
home). I walk the dog at night and think
of spots he's liked, his map of the good places.
He minds his cues and pees. "Good dog!" I praise,
uncomfortable. For us, *smell* turns to *stink*;
we are unhappy with our bodies' traces.
He does his business. I avert my gaze,
who can't return to my good places, shun
reminders that indict me, cannot say—
as I take him to be saying—"Life is fine!
I like it here." A cat, when she is done,
will cover it over and then go on her way,
fastidious, ashamed. Her way is mine.

At Èze

A city on a hill was once defiance
or piety—the effortful daily trudge
a spiting of the hordes on the plain below,
propitiation of powers above, or both
in the temple-fort. But motors have brought down
all the high places: automobiles,
trams, and trolleys leveled what the eye
still declares to be true to what the calf
muscles deny. The only cost is money
for the panoramic view that any high-rise
offers megalomania of lights
diminutive and down. The hauling up
of food, water, lumber, and stone that earned
the giddy heights and stretched the horizon but kept
scale from top to bottom is gone with the need
for safety and for prayer. It's a matter of taste,
developers' whims, and maybe an instinct—
to climb the streets some evening earns our rest;
to see the rooftops burnished in a sunset
gratifies; to feel the sky close
in San Francisco, Boston, Lisbon, Rome,
Athens or Jerusalem is to know
the strength, grace, the repose that a hill, tamed,
domesticated, gives. Men on the plains
of reason and convenience dream, at their best
of Calvary, Zion, or the Acropolis,
and in their beds flex leg muscles longing
for heights like those on which to feel at home.

Stupid

Stupid as trees, the stubborn peasants hold
with their toes extending like roots onto their old
plots, worked out, worthless, but still theirs.
They starve, a little slower than will their heirs,
but faster than their fathers did, afraid
to let go, pack up, slam closed the decayed
doors of the house and leaning barn and leave
what they know behind to set out and achieve
that better life they've dreamed about, where fields
reward improbable toil with improbable yields.

Or stupid as birds, the journeymen who wander
wherever the wind takes them, hither and yonder,
glean whatever is easy, living hard,
picking up what other men would discard.
Nothing is theirs but what they eat or wear
or carry on their backs. Fields that will bear
better for lying fallow or with new ditches
exist in a country they cannot imagine, where riches
pass from father to son by right of birth—
houses, barns, orchards, and fertile earth.

Stupid, stupid, both of them, and I
am stupid too, except that I know why.
Wisdom is neither in staying nor moving on
but in judging when to do which, and then, once gone,
not turning round to look back at the life
or prettying up the house you've left, or the wife
you've walked away from. All, movers and stayers,
birds and trees, will meet in the end, their prayers
answered, as their season at last comes round
to travel a long way on a little ground.

Courtyard

A pennon of black nylon—I suppose
thrown from a window—a pair of pantyhose
drifted down to the courtyard and hangs there,
caught in a tree, embellishing the bare
branches. The wind plays with it, twists, furls,
and smooths it. I have seen school girls,
nervous, fiddle so with their scarves, and preen,
discovering they are beautiful. The queen
of the courtyard, the tree appears to flirt with the breeze,
winds her fillet, and laughs with the other trees
that forbear to disapprove of how gaudily tricked
out she is, or complain that they were not picked . . .
Or so I hope, but questions run like cracks
in the plasterwork of these old buildings, the backs
of which overlook the courtyard: how and why
did pantyhose float down from the dirty sky
to snag on a branch? An argument, in which
some lover, absurd with rage, screamed out, "You bitch!"
and she threw what was at hand at him, and he
caught it and threw it out of the window, while she
felt more than that go, collapsed and cried,
while ghostly legs thrashed and kicked outside,
flying away as she would have liked to do . . .
Something like that must have happened. Nearly new
pantyhose don't grow on trees. The sprite
of a woman's nether half moved on the night
and grabbed at an opportunity, and still
clings to the tree. The wind's erratic will
arranges the hank of fabric, and rearranges,
making an emblem of the constant changes
by which the lower parts without the higher
writhe to the passing dictates of desire.
The North Hill quivers. I see, every day,
people carting their books and clothes away,
moving in or out in a slow dance
around the courtyard maypole that the chance

conjunction of wood and cloth has made the tree—
which makes it male. In its androgyny
we read what we can or have to, finding laws
in the rest and agitation of the gauze
the wind whips and the branch holds. No good
to worry about it, hope, fear what you would
or wouldn't do. At random, from out of the blue,
your token—a scarf, or pantyhose—falls, and you
look suddenly silly, gaudy, but sad,
and singled out. Your friends all say you're mad.
Birds avoid you. Nothing you do matters,
except to wait for time to rend to tatters
the cloth of passion, as always happens. The tree
will stand there, wait for wind and time to free
this tangle from it. All delight and grief
must pass. The furled bud springs into leaf,
dies, and is blown away. Sap falls and springs
up again and falls, but in the rings
of the tree's wooden heart, memories last
of flourishing seasons that hold an old tree fast
against new gales. What else is there to do?
Stand still, hold on, and hope to lumber through.

Rounding the Horn

1

Ticks of the mantel clock, we spawn thousands,
passing above them our shadows' milt. That whale,
oblivion, gobbles most of the fry newborn.
A few survive, thrive, to stake out rocks,
ledges, making a home. We hurry past
the addresses of those good times, and thugs, our children,
set upon us with mirror shards, stabbing,
forcing us to peer at what we've betrayed.

2

The old have ingenious diseases. A body becomes
allergic to itself, breaks into bits,
each hating the others. The family squabble
turns vicious. Helpless we hack at ourselves
like crazed sharks. Weep for peace, cry out
for them all to strike with their gleaming knives, but tears
burn the skin like lies, and the ears ring
with shrill noises no one else can hear.

3

Bulldozers, backhoes snuffle and grunt, searching
our truffle whims: let there be a hill
here, a hummock there. And then, one day,
trees are trucked in, stuck in holes, and rainbirds
spit arcs, iterating the plan.
But it keeps on going, growing, falling away
from what we intended. We learn to prune and sweat.
Whatever garden we plan, the plants plan jungle.

4

A jade fish hangs in cream jade lilies.
The man who carved it cheers us: the worked stone
of our own wit is polished by his suggestion.
But which of us could have seen in the cloudy rock
the shape of the fish that lurked there for a sculptor
to carve to? We would reach out to feed,

but at its safety glass, among the sedge
of finger smudges, our starving hands are stopped.

5
The bags we routed through LAG may have gone to LAX,
may return Thursday, or never. Relax, the suits,
shirts, socks were more than we needed. Razors
are on sale everywhere, and wash-and-wear
will keep us decent. We travel light and smile
at youngsters in airports with mountains of matched luggage.
They are innocents, fools. Someone should have advised them.
Who had the heart, the heartlessness, the nerve?

6
Time drips like a deep wound, and faint,
I would lie down like Antaeus to soak strength
from the earth. Even the undead, dragging coffins
from country to country survived the break of dawns
stretched out, hung on as if to a new neck.
But earth has nothing left to give, gives out.
In dust storms, animals drop. From the bed of my youth,
I rise exhausted by dreams I cannot remember.

7
Wind and lightning for wisdom? The Chinese
had odd notions. Illumination, of course,
and no one can grasp the wind. But storms are wrong,
too intuitive, and a threat to the foolish
wisdom ought to shelter. Better, the whale.
Its song could span an ocean and kept the herd
whole—until propellor noise shredded
the conversation to dirges I recognize.

8
Sailing the furniture through storms, we braved
the shallows of the night, the deck awash

in brain waves' breakers, as beacons of light
shadowed nightmare perils. The captain clung
to the binnacle like a pillow. The dangerous cargo
shifted down in the hold. Who then could imagine
this warehouse where we swap tales with shore strangers
of bizarre adventures, all of them probably true?

9
Feeding upon the garden of their innards,
the foraminifera need only warmth, light,
and the water's salts, thrive for six months,
and then explode into thousands of new selves,
leaving behind tests that make limestone.
The pyramids are their monuments more than the pharaohs'—
humans whose friends could turn away. Love founders,
and elaborate needs betray our conditional lives.

10
Sporting in the sea, their sleek dazzle
of fur breaks the surface, and then they dive
to reappear twenty yards down the beach.
Children who stand and watch them imagine the seals'
fun a free swim that goes on forever.
We know better, having learned from our lives'
endless and opposite cravings how they swim
between their bellies' pangs and their lungs' burning.

11
Not monsters, but strangers who have retreated
for safety—or to sulk—down so deep
nothing that threatened them can bear the pressure,
huge, deformed by the bottoms they rule, they appear
only by some mischance—snagged in a cable.
We call them ugly to mask our fear and envy
of an adaptation few of us in the shallows
could make to their ugly occasion, whatever it was.

12
Crystal Lagoon, the Franco-Irish Bombshell
with hair the color of sand was innocent once,
a cheerleader with Coral Strand, waved pom-poms,
and shouted "Gauguin, Go!" Those days are gone;
too old to be a B-girl now, she sells
souvenirs in the islands where AID
distributes IUDs to native girls
no more imaginable than our escape.

13
The fire under the pu-pu platter gutters;
our ribs congeal. With the last of the tea we read
apothegms tucked in our cookies: "Hungers are always
sated." Dull, we long only for sleep.
Likewise in love. Our eyes, our imaginations
are noble. We sit down to an emperor's banquet.
Our small stomachs raise their peasants' rebellion,
deposing us. The waiter wants to go home.

14
There, on the ocean floor, ships may ride
in impossible attitudes, toe-dancer poses,
stand on their noses, or roll over like kittens
and dream what they like in the weatherless aimlessness.
We think of our own manifests and, seasick,
fear their gloom and silence less than the freedom
catastrophe offers. Richly encrusted, they sport,
make pets of monsters, have learned how to settle.

15
At the tempting islands, you jump ship to loll
the gentle life on the beach in a lavalava
or drink rum on the rim of a dead volcano,
but soon boredom bites like gnats, and the rash
act can itch like the devil asleep in the crater.

Blinded by all those breasts, you scan the sea
in search of a ship, as if you had money or hope
of talking the captain into a free ride back.

16
Holes in the fabric where the moths attack
vulnerable places dirt has touched . . .
I eat, drink, sweat, roll on the floor,
and like critics, crows, they come, greedy for sins,
to nibble with their small mouths at the fibers
wound around me, shredding the finery
that cost so much to rags, tattered pretensions,
a gauzy net of ruined hopes, a shroud.

17
"The island beckons. Beyond the first glare
of sunlight on the coral reefs, white dunes,
and gentle meadows, lush thickets promise
succulent fruits we have never tasted, treasures
we cannot imagine . . . " The journal ends there.
Hacking into that underbrush, good men,
lost, have drowned in quicksand, cursing the peaks
of delight for which they had left the plains of comfort.

18
Lovable, huge, the last right whale will breach,
all that shining lonely tonnage turned
to a heavy joke. Who has not stared in the tub
at his own sad bulk to ask the same
sodden question—what was it all for
to come to this? The ignorant distant toes
pucker as always, having learned at least
that warm water cools. It's time to get out.

19
This island once was promising. The find

caused shares and hopes to rise and bright young men
to volunteer, their eyes fixed upon fortunes
aching to be made here. Look at us now,
on sagging verandahs, drunk, awaiting the steamer's
demands and reprimands from the home office
or news from other islands where poor bastards
reply in kind to all our cheerful lies.

20
The febrile tropics recede. The islands, astern,
fall away below the horizon, as languor
falls from the limbs. Winds freshen. The mind clears.
Dolphins play in the sea. Health is to wake
and not even remark at the absence of pain.
Gulls, greedy for garbage, cavort, amuse,
and startle, meaning that land is somewhere ahead:
home. The heart throbs with the ship's screws.

21
Land legs are easy to get back.
The flat, prosy fields and reason's pavement
teach at every step the certitudes
townsmen are willing to live by and die by.
But stopping is risky. Stand still and look up
at foliage in the wind, at clouds in the sky,
and in dizziness, a fit of the tropic ailment,
a meadow melts to a sea running four feet high.

22
What young men learn and what some grown men know
bleaches out in the glare of hot afternoons
in front of the post office or hardware store
where old men settle. Their faces show more
than they and the local decencies care to admit
of wilder adventures than our neat village squares
can compass, except as a last indifferent roost
for whatever they were that must come to rest somewhere.

74

23
Madness earns a place for itself. The town
learns its manners as habit scabs over fear.
I go to the bank or store or walk the beach
and get neither more nor less than a brisk "Good morning,"
except from young boys, silent, uneasy, each
supposing I know his secret, can see his yearning,
or feel his defiance—that he'll do better than I.
They turn away from me, my life, my warning.

24
Depression, whiskey, diarrhea, rage,
and late at night, a poring over maps . . .
The old symptoms return. I pace my cage
like a jungle cat so long in the zoo, the lust
for escape has faded away. Assume a lapse
of diligence, a door left open just
that longed-for moment; would he still make the try,
or give it up, stop pacing at last, and die?

25
When appetite dies, the fear of death also
dies. Home, apparently brave and good,
aping the angels, we take an abstemious crumb
and gag. With seeming grace we walk in the slow
steps of saints or invalids. The blood,
thinned in the tropics, runs pure as water from
the eyes of icons weeping miracles. Free
at last of our clamorous mouths and tyrannical organs,
we pass for pious, although our deity
is nausea or hate. In our private jargons,
we pray, curse the world's unyielding crust—
and prayer, sooner or later, is answered. The earth,
making its late amends for the trauma of birth,
opens, receives, quiets our grumbling dust.

Garbage

An etymologic mystery, garbage
is, nevertheless, a teleologic
likelihood of appalling obviousness,
the tendency of

things to turn sooner or later into junk,
scrap, detritus, everywhere evident—
not just in use objects and ornaments, but
ideas and people,

even saints (poor Christopher, for example)
even in the gods (Mazda's a bulb, a car).
The priests of garbage display sectarian
animus, whether

their faith be in the ancient quartet of air,
earth, fire, and water, burning, burying, or
dumping fragrant scowsful into deep places
where we can't see it,

or whether they hold with the oriental
theories of reincarnation, and sort out
aluminum cans, newsprint, rags, and the like,
saving organic

wastes for the compost heap, in the serene hope
of another life—or deviation from
the condition of garbage to which time pulls
with the furies' force

whatever intricate work we do or are
in the dump's despite. The distillate of years
stands in a dozen liquor cartons in the premonitory

guise of the garbage it will soon enough be.
Papers, books, pictures—I shall store some, ship some,
throw much away, but I have been hunting for
some object of worth,

pawing through my own litter, as a cat will,
in the hope I may find some treasure, some prize
better than my own dirt. Museums suggest
it happens sometimes,

that somehow or other there can be reprieves
from the great inferno (itself, condemned as
polluting the air). But curators err too,
humans that they are,

so we can all hope. I try to believe in
a God, sifting through all this rubble, and pray
that his hand, gloved and undoubtedly filthy,
discovering me

may hesitate and, in that instant's pause, let
me imagine what He remembers—that I
was once supposed to fit somewhere, that I was
not always garbage.

Dickens' Inkwell, Etc.

Dickens' inkwell, Jefferson's walking stick,
the door of Tom Paine's house, Caruso's belt buckle . . .
    What powers have they? They cannot enlighten us,
however much we stare at them (too dumb to pose
        questions, too smart to admit a belief
in saints' relics), or heal; there must be, nevertheless,
        something in the careers of objects to tease us,
to turn our abstracted heads. If works, words or music
        or pictures, are issue, these association
items are friends, chosen cronies whose testimony
        is quiet and quite different from what a man's
children are likely to say. These inanimate chums
        are like our own, what we reach for, first
things of the morning—a wallet, a pen, a pocket knife
        without which we're naked. Who hasn't lost
such a token, totem, and foraged drawers as an uneasy bitch
        whose pup has been sold, is gone? And how do we
explain this to the dog who, anyway, is right,
        snuffles the closets, the cellar steps over
and over, looking to us for comfort we can hardly
        offer, with our children disappearing
too, there one day and the next different, gone,
        forgiving (we hope), even friendly, but not
the youngsters we held in our arms, taught, fed, played with . . . ?
        And we are left to play with these toys for small
comforts: I have a gold fountain pen, a cheap
        nameplate from my first desk job, a cigar cutter
in chrome a girl gave me . . . What would they signify
        to the collector (assuming—a hell of a lot—
I'm ever worth collecting)? Little, indeed, which is all
        a friend should say. Less well bred, we stare,
inquiring *What was he like?* or hoping his quality
        might still inhere, accessible if not
to the sight, then, to the touch as in a medal blessed
        by the pope, the personalty a vessel for
the personality, itself. It must be so!

But then what we call the civilized world turns
primitive, dangerous, our rooms, streets become
    a bracken of bondings and marriages. Ghosts lurk
the air like germs from which only our ignorance
    protects us, and our thick skins. Or make it a schoolroom
with each of us sitting at desks in the slanting afternoon sun,
    the carved initials and agonized doodles alive,
souls writhing like snakes, the chair a seethe of sweat
    of the venerable questions (if only our dumb
butts could perceive the answers soaked in the knowing wood!).
    There is some rudimentary tingle at these
keepsakes, the matter of men who matter. My cat knows
    the ceremony better than I do.
She rubs against a chair, a piano leg, or mine,
    marking with the glands behind her ears
HERS. Our noses are much less acute (thank God—
    we couldn't stand to live in what must smell
like a subway car) as is our love: our ineptitudes
    fit together tolerably well.
To put an extreme case, whose pipe would you smoke?
    The heavy glass protects us from the object's
taint as much as it from us and what we think
    is reverence. With savage energy
we clean out the closets, the drawers of our dead,
    keep back only the watches, cuff links, studs,
and perhaps a few of the better ties, but get rid of the rest.
    This gold pen will survive, then, being gold,
impervious to tarnish, rust, or even my mortal
    and un-Midas touch. Josephine's tiara
in Van Cleef's window fetches more for her having worn it
    (and she, thereby, becomes a knickknack), but we
live mostly in base metals, in wood, in cloth,
    crockery, glass, and plastic. I have imagined
the hand of God sifting a midden to find my wreck.
    Closer to the truth is the homelier question—
what will happen to my pocket knife? Will friends,

readers, or even my children want to keep
some tangy relic of mine? These goods of our lives
    exhort us to goodness for our sakes and their own.
The spoil of the auction houses is all from defeats
    in obscure wars of taste and virtue.
What else in the world is worth fighting for or about?

Poison

There are always sounds at night. I hear them now,
think of the house on the cape, and remember how
the mice (or were they chipmunks?) carried on
at night inside the walls. We bought D-Con
to set out for them. And that poison may
be in there still. I never found a way
to throw it out safely. The dump wasn't
right or the woods behind the barn where a pheasant
or gull could have gotten into it, and I
had no quarrel with them. Rats are sly,
elect a taster, they say, who, hungry or bold,
tries new food while all the others hold
a vigil, waiting to see if he lives. Mice
may not be quite so clever or so precise,
but they left droppings I found the next year
mixed with the pellets, warnings to stay clear.
I think of the poison there behind the wall
of the bedroom where we listened to the small
feet or sharp teeth scratching the repose
we broke ourselves, less circumspect than those
cautious rodents. Terse instructions said
they'd eat, thirst, flee, and that there'd be no dead
bodies decomposing. A clean demise!
But what about the crow whose tainted prize
those mice might be? I never thought of that,
or of the possibility a cat
could eat a dying mouse. The A.E.C.
cares better for its poisons, I hope, than we.
     A continent away, that room is still
the shape of any room the dark can fill,
and that wall backs on any bed. I strain
to hear that old life scratching. In my brain,
predators stalk, the poisons wait, and traps
with baited jaws are yawning in my naps.
In my remorse, those vermin play, and I
feel old loathing but identify

a different target now. In that old house
there was room and enough for us and a little mouse.
To go buy poisons in a hardware store
and bring them home . . . I ask myself, what for?
The hope was for perfection, but the fact
was stained and staining, as the field mice tracked
their dying through our lives. I feel a twinge
of misdirected tender feeling, cringe,
and realize what we killed, trying to rid
our lives of harmless scratchings, what we did.
Fear grips me now. I can't get rid of it.
Like poison, it remains, the rodents' wit.

Rampal/ Flute

Lighter than air, updrafts of the spirit,
the notes of a phrase can turn abruptly burly
as the lights that glint on its metal can stretch out
and turn to tempered blades.

His chest is broad as a beer-truck-driver's helper's;
somewhere in the andante it appears
no embellishment to suppose him chinning himself
on the flute he holds, hangs onto, about to ascend
big-top high. Assuredly, he shall,
if heaven is sane. The luggage of harpists is heavy,
cumberous as our sins, but this aspiration,
inspired expiration, our admiration
recognizes at once, as his breath controls
the celebrations at which our joy would gasp.

In the splash, the shine, the daring of his rising,
he bears the prayers of all our burning lungs—
not least, that he may, in the gaudy wake he trails,
take us along.

After the Concert

Julliard Quartet, Berkeley, February 16, 1977

Listen, Mann, for I've just listened to you
up on the stage, playing with three new
musicians you've picked up. It isn't the same
Julliard Quartet. You've kept the name
but lost the recognizable sound. The blend
isn't what it was. What happened, friend?
Did they abandon you? Get sick or die?
Or just get tired of touring and playing? Why,
for that matter, am I in this Berkeley hall?
We've both put on some weight. Your hair was all
black once. And I've gone rather to seed.
Partners change, yes. And you don't need
me to recite the obvious. What we know
is in the music. You used to take the slow
movements with the richness of content . . .
Your present cellist saws on his instrument
the same notes, but a parody now, a refrain,
barely an echo of those first bars of our sane
and sanguine youth. The records from years back
are beautiful still. But painful. The attack,
the swell, the modulation . . . What do they,
these youngsters, know? Oh, I have heard you play
such harmonies as few marriages match.
But music dies. Even the records scratch.
And there you are. The second violin
is off a half a beat. The cello comes in
rasping . . . Or is the trouble with my ear?
Have I, somewhere from Miami to Boston to here,
lost the sense of the score? It could well be
that I'm the one unstrung and out of key.
Or both of us are. Davidovsky's nervous
dissonances scrape and, jangling, serve as
cris de coeur, or cries that come from the gut.
But even Beethoven seems distracted. What

are we doing here? What has become of us?
Connection drops away. The parting was
painful, of course. Did you all quarrel, shout,
or did the worm of boredom find you out
so that you took for granted that great gift
of personal harmony? And you are left
playing with strangers to strangers those old scores.
I remember once you used to take encores.
You bow now to applause you haven't earned.
And I salute you, having myself learned
what nerve it takes. Once there was delight;
the object now is getting through the night.
Audiences don't know much. We're through.
They can go home. We do what we have to do,
professionals, remembering the truth
of promise, of talent, of joy, of love, of youth.
I grieve, but I salute you, what you were
and what you are. God bless, God spare you, sir.

Prospector

Pauci veniunt ad senectutem.

These buttes and obdurate chimneys are the remains
of what were once unremarkable valleys.
Just so, the craggy sentences survive
of stern men from the East with chipped noses
and marble eyes, our cicerones. Who
would declaim against the years of wind and weather?
But this dry desert air ages us all
to their indifferent attention. California
or bust?—the odds are equal and the appeal
is about the same, partner. By luck or desert,
some hard-mined nuggets of ours will make it
into collectors' cases of rare issues
or even, worn smooth, into the pockets
of ordinary folks, their small change.

Going West

Behind are those disasters of civilized
ambition which I flee, selfish and eager
for life in undemanding California
    where there are trivial

men and women who are all pleasant figments
of each other's imaginations—which is
what we'd all like the nerve to be, protected
    by miles, plains, mountains from

the distresses of our old imperatives,
ethical and cultural, the hurts of such
fussy Atlantic notions as honor or
    consequent self-esteem.

Here, where only a few cute missions are old,
where, in the sunshine of the present moment,
fugitives can thrive, flourish like lettuces,
    our faults and pretensions

diminished seemingly, for the only fault
worth the fretting about is that of the earth
we walk, not living and not building (those are
    proud words) but satisfied

to improvise for a while as in a country
where there are no cold seasons demanding thrift,
patience, the responsible postponement of
    all gratifications.

Winters and rocky soil with its promises
made for what we called stern character, taught us
to hold on, but here, no past, no future
    but a present like fruit

always in season lets us let go the tics
of Eastern time. I play with grown-up children,
frivolous, contemptibly happy as I
    hope, myself, to become.

Mess

Why pretend a drawing room? The animals roam it
    like a pampas, pee on the couch, and shred the haunch
of the straw elephant; I am an even messier beast
    than dog or cat. My shirt's been on that chair
nearly a week, the beret on the table about ten days.
    All of this ought to appear on the page—
the implication of servants is false, the suggestion of order,
    horse shit. Any poem born in this room
ought to look out on the world through a filthy window painted
    shut years ago (excuse my excuse),
scurry for cover, a roach in the sudden light, gurgle
    of old pipes in the night, hiss and bang.
Let the litter live, in the name of cranky pride:
    if company come, let them see how it is.
The squeamish, or those with too sharp eyes, will not come back,
    and no loss—blindness and kindness, welcome,
sit wherever they will. I'll rinse a glass
    and fill it with cheap gin. We'll drink to grandeur.